ICE CREAM

Copyright © 1989 American Teacher Publications

Published by Raintree Publishers Limited Partnership

Library of Congress number: 89-3931

Library of Congress Cataloging in Publication Data.

Keller, Stella.
   The story of ice cream / Stella Keller.

   (Real readers)
   Summary: The anecdotal history of ice cream, for beginning readers, traces the treat from the ices eaten by Emperor Nero to modern day ice cream factories.
   1. Ice cream, ices, etc.—Juvenile literature. [1. Ice cream, ices, etc.] I. Title.
II. Series.
TX795.K45   1989   637'.4—dc20   89-3931

ISBN 0-8172-3523-X

1 2 3 4 5 6 7 8 9 0   93 92 91 90 89

REAL READERS

ICE CREAM

by Stella Keller
illustrated by John Holm

Raintree Publishers
Milwaukee

Ice cream is fun to eat. Today, when you want to eat ice cream, you can go to a store and get it.

Long ago, people did not have good ways to get ice. They did not have **freezers** to keep things cold. For a long time it was so hard to make cold treats, that just kings and queens got to eat them.

How did people of long ago make ice cream and other cold treats?

This is how they did it.

About 2,000 years ago, a man named Nero was the Emperor in Rome. Nero wanted to eat a cold treat.

How did Nero get his cold treat?

There was ice on the tops of the hills outside Rome. Nero would send people to get the ice. After they got the ice, they would run all the way back to Rome. Then Nero's cooks mixed the ice with **fruit** and **honey**.

It was not ice cream. But Nero liked this cold treat very much.

Other people in other places liked to eat cold treats, too. About 700 years ago, a man named Marco Polo went on a trip from his home in Italy. He went to China.

In China, he got to eat something good. It was made with ice, like the treat Nero ate, but it had something new in it. The something new was **milk**. Back then, people in China got milk from an animal called the yak.

How did the people in China make this treat?

They put fruit and **sugar** in a pot. Then they mixed in crushed ice. They added milk. Then they mixed up all the fruit, sugar, milk, and ice.

When Marco Polo went back to Italy, he told his friends all about this new, sweet treat.

About 500 years ago, some cooks in Italy, France, and England made cold, sweet treats. The treats were like the one Marco Polo had in China. But now the cooks added something new.

How did the cooks make the treats?

They added not just milk, but **cream** to ice, fruit, and sugar. They made ice cream!

Back then ice cream was very hard to make. People had to mix the ice, fruit, sugar, and cream for a very, very long time. It was very hard for them to get all the ice they needed to make ice cream and to keep it cold.

Kings and queens got to eat ice cream. Sometimes, the cooks who made the ice cream got to eat a little bit, too. But other people did not get to have ice cream at that time.

Then, about 300 years ago, a man named Procope had a shop in France. Mr. Procope made ice cream in the shop. He made ice cream not just for kings and queens, but for all the people.

How did Mr. Procope make ice cream?

Mr. Procope needed a way to keep lots of ice cream in his shop. He did not have freezers like we do today. But he did have a way to keep ice cream cold. He got big boxes and filled them with ice. The ice helped keep the ice cream cold for a long time.

He made ice cream in many **flavors**. He made **chocolate**, **vanilla**, **strawberry**, and rose-flavored ice cream, too!

As time passed, more and more people got to eat ice cream. At last, ice cream came to America. About 200 years ago, America's first President, George Washington, liked to eat ice cream.

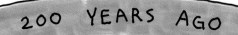

200 YEARS AGO

George
Washington

How did people make ice cream in George Washington's time?

First, they mixed the cream, flavors, and sugar in a little pot. Sometimes, they mixed in **eggs**, too. Next, they got a big pot and put ice in it. Then they put the little pot in the big pot.

Two people had to work together. One would beat the mix in the little pot. The other would shake the big pot. It was still very hard to make ice cream!

Then, in 1846, a woman in America made a new **machine** to make ice cream. This woman was named Nancy Johnson.

How did Nancy Johnson make ice cream?

Nancy Johnson's machine had a little pot that fit inside a big pot. The cream mix went in the little pot. The ice went in the big pot. At the top was a crank.

If someone turned the crank, it beat the mix in the little pot and it made the ice in the big pot shake. Now it was not as hard to make ice cream. Many people got ice cream machines. They used the new machines to make ice cream at home.

But soon, people did not have to make ice cream to eat it. In 1851, a man named Jacob Fussell was selling milk and cream in Baltimore. He had too much cream to sell. So, he came up with a plan.

He used the cream that he could not sell to make ice cream. People liked to get ice cream from him. Soon, he was selling more ice cream than cream or milk! He was selling all the ice cream he could make!

How did Jacob Fussell make all the ice cream he needed to sell?

This is how he did it. He got some people together. They used machines like Nancy Johnson's. Many people working together could make lots of ice cream to sell. This was the first ice cream **factory**.

Today, much of the ice cream we eat is made in an ice cream factory. But people can make ice cream at home, too. Some people still make ice cream in machines very much like Nancy Johnson's machine.

Now, you can get ice cream in many places. You can go to a store and get ice cream from the freezer and take it home. You can get an ice cream cone and eat it in a shop. You can make ice cream at home if you have an ice cream machine.

You can eat ice cream in a cup, or in a cone, or on a stick. You can eat it with fruit or with cake. But the best way to eat ice cream is with a friend!

Sharing the Joy of Reading

Beginning readers enjoy reading books on their own. Reading a book is a worthwhile activity in and of itself for a young reader. However, a child's reading can be even more rewarding if it is shared. This sharing can enhance your child's appreciation — both of the book and of his or her own abilities.

- Now that your child has read **Ice Cream**, you can help extend your child's reading experience by encouraging him or her to:

- Retell the story or key concepts presented in this story in his or her own words. The retelling can be oral or written.

- Create a picture of a favorite character, event, or concept from this book.

- Express his or her own ideas and feelings about the subject of this book and other things he or she might want to know about this subject.

Here is an activity that you can do together to help extend your child's appreciation of this book: You and your child can make a sweet-tasting frozen treat. Prepare your child's favorite frozen juice with a little less water than usual. Pour the juice into small paper cups and place the cups in the freezer. When the juice begins to harden, set wooden sticks or plastic spoons in the cups for handles. After the juice solidifies, peel off the paper and enjoy.

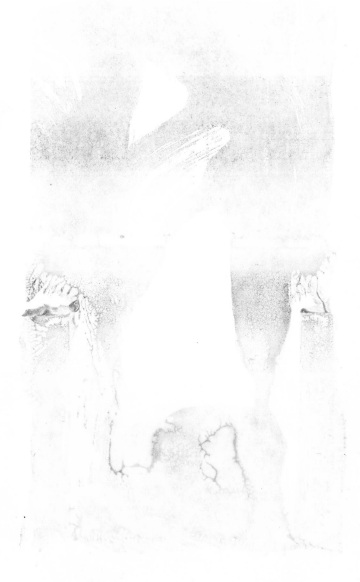

ICE CREAM

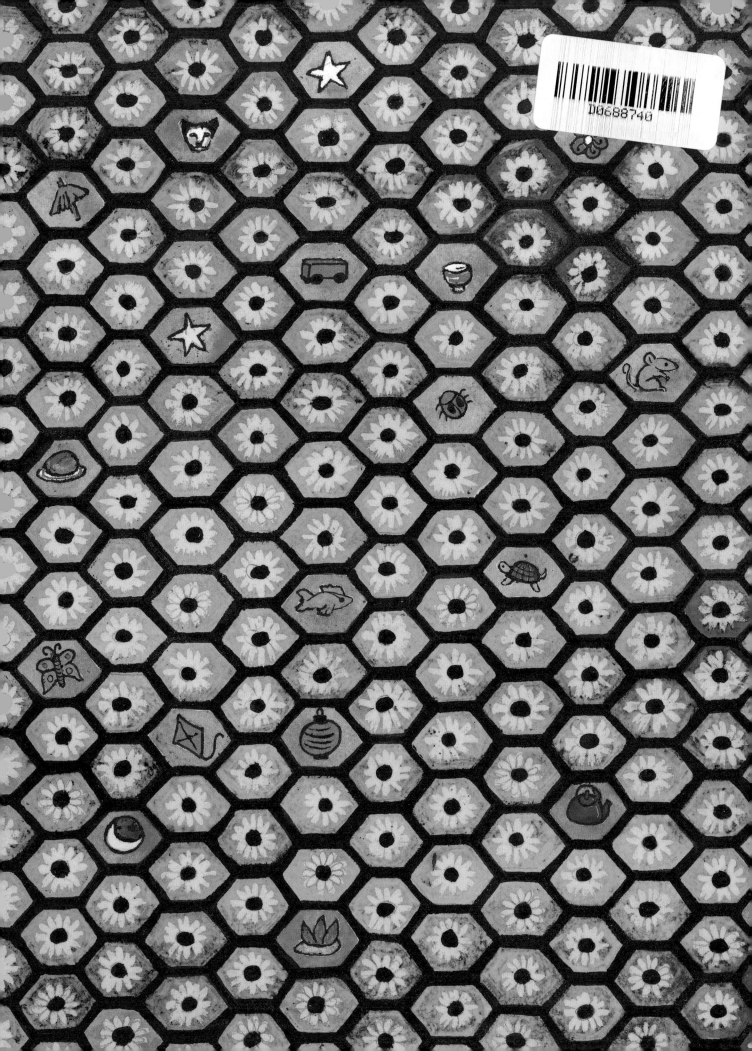

Chinese
and English
Nursery Rhymes

LITTLE MOUSE
AND OTHER CHARMING CHINESE RHYMES

FAYE-LYNN WU
illustrated by
KIEREN DUTCHER

TUTTLE Publishing

Tokyo | Rutland, Vermont | Singapore

ABOUT TUTTLE
"Books to Span the East and West"

Our core mission at Tuttle Publishing is to create books which bring people together one page at a time. Tuttle was founded in 1832 in the small New England town of Rutland, Vermont (USA). Our fundamental values remain as strong today as they were then—to publish best-in-class books informing the English-speaking world about the countries and peoples of Asia. The world has become a smaller place today and Asia's economic, cultural and political influence has expanded, yet the need for meaningful dialogue and information about this diverse region has never been greater. Since 1948, Tuttle has been a leader in publishing books on the cultures, arts, cuisines, languages and literatures of Asia. Our authors and photographers have won numerous awards and Tuttle has published thousands of books on subjects ranging from martial arts to paper crafts. We welcome you to explore the wealth of information available on Asia at **www.tuttlepublishing.com**.

Published by Tuttle Publishing, an imprint of Periplus Editions (HK) Ltd.

www.tuttlepublishing.com

Copyright © 2010 by Faye-Lynn Wu
Illustrations © 2010 by Kieren Dutcher

ISBN 978-0-8048-4999-9
(Previously published as under ISBN 978-0-8048-4094-1, CIP Data No. 2009031567)

First edition
22 21 20 19 18   4 3 2 1   1801EP

Printed in Hong Kong

Distributed by

North America, Latin America & Europe
Tuttle Publishing
364 Innovation Drive
North Clarendon, VT 05759-9436 U.S.A.
Tel: 1 (802) 773-8930
Fax: 1 (802) 773-6993
info@tuttlepublishing.com
www.tuttlepublishing.com

Asia Pacific
Berkeley Books Pte. Ltd.
61 Tai Seng Avenue #02-12
Singapore 534167
Tel: (65) 6280-1330
Fax: (65) 6280-6290
inquiries@periplus.com.sg
www.periplus.com

TUTTLE PUBLISHING® is a registered trademark of Tuttle Publishing, a division of Periplus Editions (HK) Ltd.

To my husband, Alex, and children, Benjamin and Rachel,
for their love, patience, and support.
—FW

To Dan, Sophie and William.
I couldn't have done it without you!
—KD

Our sincere thanks to our family, friends, and colleagues in the CD song production—Madeleine King, a fantastic musician, for her creative songwriting and lovely music; the singers, PJ (Paul) Robinson, Caroline Portante, Adella K. Cho, Cathy (Lan Qi) Li, Shihua Liu, and Hui Qiao Wu; Menna Stern for her technical support; and John Carlstroem and Siu-mui Woo for their support behind the scenes.

Introduction

When my son was born, I read him Mother Goose rhymes and sang my favorite childhood songs in Chinese to ease my own homesickness. Not only did I have fun learning the English rhymes with my son, but I also passed my Chinese heritage down to him through singing and acting out my old favorites. I can still see his sleepy face and hear his childish voice begging for more rhymes: "Sing, mommy, sing."

Children naturally love music and verse, so it is no wonder that nursery rhymes appeal to us as children and stay with us throughout our lives. What could be a more enjoyable way to learn a different culture and language than through rhymes and songs?

Bugs, trains, counting: we've paired the rhymes by shared themes, so for each, there's a Chinese rhyme and an English rhyme to delight in. We invite young readers and adults to explore the magic of children's rhymes and the universal quality of the shared world of childhood. We also provide notes throughout the book so that you can learn more about Chinese culture.

Whether you are a native Chinese speaker or English speaker, you can learn the rhymes and songs—simply follow the words as you sing, or join in the chorus on the audio CD.

Enjoy!

Faye-Lynn Wu and Kieren Dutcher

Contents

Rig-a-Jig-Jig

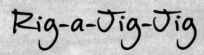

As I was walking down the street,
Down the street,
Down the street,
A pretty girl (boy) I chanced to meet
Heigh–ho, heigh–ho, heigh–ho.

Rig–a–jig–jig and away we go, away we go
Away we go
Rig–a–jig–jig and away we go
Heigh–ho, heigh–ho, heigh–ho.

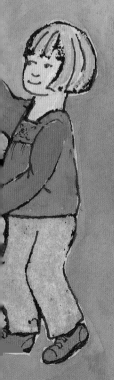

When We Are Together
当我们同在一起
dāng wǒ men tóng zài yì qǐ

当我们同在一起
dāng wǒ men tóng zài yì qǐ
When we are together

在一起, 在一起
zài yì qǐ, zài yì qǐ
Together, together

当我们同在一起
dāng wǒ men tóng zài yì qǐ
When we are together

其快乐无比
qí kuài lè wú bǐ
We are so happy

你对着我笑嘻嘻
nǐ duì zhē wǒ xiào xī xī
Smiling, you look at me

我对着你笑哈哈
wǒ duì zhe nǐ xiào hā hā
Laughing, I look back at you

当我们同在一起
dāng wǒ men tóng zài yì qǐ
When we are together

其快乐无比
qí kuài lè wú bǐ
We are so happy.

Kites Go Up

The kites go up,
the kites go down,
In and around,
all over the town.

The children run
and jump and play,
Because they love
a windy day.

Jumping Rope
跳绳
tiào shéng

绳子抡的团团转
shéng zi lun de túan túan zhuàn
The jump rope turns round and round.

妹妹进来跳跳看
mèi mei jìn lái tiào tiào kàn
Little sister, please come and try jumping in

一二三四五六七
yī èr sān sì wǔ liù qī
One two three four five six seven

跳得过的尽你玩
tiào de guò dē jìn nǐ wán
Play as long as you can jump

一二三四五六七
yī èr sān sì wǔ liù qī
One two three four five six seven

跳不过的就要换
tiào bú guò dē jiù yào huàn
If you can't, then wait your turn.

Do you know ...

Kites were invented in China about 2,000 years ago. They were originally designed to use in wars to spy on enemies or send messages. Later, kites were used for fun.

As I Was Going Along

As I was going along, along
A-singing a comical song, song, song,
The lane I went down was so long, long, long
And the song that I sang was so long, long, long,
And so I went singing along.

Tune on a Bamboo Flute

紫竹调
zǐ zhú diào

一根紫竹直苗苗
yì gēn zǐ zhú zhí miáo miáo
One straight bamboo stick

送给宝宝做管箫
sòng gěi bǎo bǎo zùo guǎn xiāo
Makes a pipe for the baby

箫儿对正口
xiāor duì zhèng kǒu
Lining up the flute with the mouth

口儿对正箫
kǒur duì zhèng xiāo
Putting the mouth on the flute

箫中吹出时新调
xiāo zhōng chuī chū shí xīn diào
The flute creates new tunes

小宝宝一滴一滴学会了
xiāo bǎo bǎo yì dī yì dī xué huì liǎo
Step by step little baby learns to play

小宝宝一滴一滴学会了
xiāo bǎo bǎo yì dī yì dī xué huì liǎo
Step by step little baby learns to play.

Ladybug

Ladybug, ladybug
Fly away home
Your house is on fire
Your children all gone.

All but one,
and her name is Ann
She crept under
the frying pan.

Little Bugs
小虫虫
xiǎo chóng chóng

虫虫虫虫飞
chóng chóng chóng chóng fēi
Bugs fly

两只虫虫斗斗嘴
liǎng zhī chóng chóng dòu dòu zuǐ
Two bugs fight

大虫跟着走
dà chóng gēn zhe zǒu
The big bug follows

小虫要娘背
xiǎo chóng yào niáng bēi
The baby bug wants to be carried.

I Am a Little Bird
我是只小小鸟
wǒ shì zhī xiǎo xiǎo niǎo

我是只小小鸟
I am a little bird
wǒ shì zhī xiǎo xiǎo niǎo

飞就飞，叫就叫
fēi jiù fēi, jiào jiù jiào
Soaring and chirping

自由逍遥
zì yóu xiāo yáo
Freely and happily

我不知有忧愁
wǒ bù zhī yǒu yōu chóu
I have no sadness

我不知有烦恼
wǒ bù zhī yǒu fán nǎo
I have no worries

只是爱欢笑
zhǐ shì ài huān xiào
I only love to laugh.

Birds

Once I saw a little bird
Come hop, hop, hop
And I cried, "Little bird,
Will you stop, stop, stop?"
I was going to the window
To say, How do you do?
But then he shook his little tail
And away he flew.

Do you know ...

The Chinese admire nature. These are the plants that represent each of the four seasons:

✳ Spring...orchid 春兰 **chūn lán**
✳ Summer...lotus 夏荷 **xià hé**
✳ Autumn...chrysanthemum 秋菊 **qīu jú**
✳ Winter...plum blossom 冬梅 **dōng méi**

Can you find these flowers in the garden?

One Two Three Four Five

One two three four five,
Once I caught a fish alive
Six seven eight nine ten,
Then I let it go again.

Why did you let it go?
Because it bit my finger so.
Which finger did it bite?
The little finger on the right.

One Two Three, Climb Up the Mountain
一二三，爬上山
yī èr sān pá shàng shān

一二三，爬上山
yī èr sān pá shàng shān
One two three, climb up the mountain

四五六，翻跟头
sì wǔ liù fān gēn tóu
Four five six, somersault

七八九，拍皮球
qī bā jiǔ pāi pí qiú
Seven eight nine, bounce the ball

伸出两只手
shēn chū liǎng zhī shǒu
Put out two hands

十个手指头
shí ge shǒu zhǐ tóu
Ten fingers in all.

Do you know ...

Everywhere in the world, people use their hands to communicate with each other. This is how Chinese children count on their hands from 1 to 10.

Can you do it? Is it different from the way you count on your hands?

13

I Hear Thunder

I hear thunder
I hear thunder
Hark, don't you?
Hark, don't you?

Pitter-patter rain drops
Pitter-patter rain drops
I'm wet through
So are you.

The Rain Is Coming
下雨歌
xià yǔ gē

淅沥淅沥哗啦哗啦
xīlī xīlī huālā huālā
Sili-sili wha-la wha-la

雨下来了
yǔ xià lái le
The rain is coming down

我的妈妈来了, 来了
wǒ de māma lái le lái le
My mom is coming, coming

拿着一把伞
ná zhe yì bǎ sǎn
Holding an umbrella

淅沥淅沥哗啦哗啦
xīlī xīlī huālā huālā
Sili-sili wha-la wha-la

啦啦啦
lā lā lā
La la la.

14

I Love Little Pussy

I love little Pussy
Her coat is so warm
And if I don't hurt her
She'll do me no harm.

So I'll not pull her tail
Nor drive her away
But Pussy and I
Very gently will play.

Little Kitten
小猫咪
xiǎo māo mī

小猫咪
xiǎo māo mī
Little kitten

过河西
guò hé xī
Crossing the West River

跟奶奶
gēn nǎi nǎi
Following grandma

吃东西
chī dōng xī
To find some food

扯花布
chě huā bù
Playing with beautiful fabric

做花衣
zuò huā yī
To make fancy clothing.

15

Hickory Dickory Dock

Hickory dickory dock
The mouse went up the clock.

The clock struck one
The mouse ran down

Hickory dickory dock.
Hickory dickory dock.

Little Mouse
小老鼠
xiǎo lǎo shǔ

小老鼠上灯台
xiǎo lǎo shǔ shàng dēng tái
The little mouse climbed up the lamp

偷油吃
tōu yóu chī
To find some oil to nibble

下不来
xià bù lái
Can't get down

喵喵喵
miāo miāo miāo
Meow, meow, meow

猫来了
māo lái le
Here came the cat

叽哩咕噜滚下来
jī lī gū lū gǔn xià lái
Ji-li-gu-lu down fell the mouse.

Do you know ...

Chinese people use paper to make colorful lanterns. Long ago, people hung lanterns to chase away evil spirits. Today people hang lanterns for good luck and decoration. At celebrations for New Year, other holidays, and weddings, you see beautiful lanterns on the streets, in parks, and at temples.

The little mice are too scared to come down. Can you help the little mice find their mother?

17

To Market, to Market

To market, to market, to buy a fat pig;
Home again, home again, jiggetty-jig.

To market, to market, to buy a fat hog;
Home again, home again, jiggetty-jog.

To market, to market, to buy a plum bun;
Home again, home again, market is done.

Tricycle
三轮车
sān lún chē

三轮车
sān lún chē
Tricycle

跑得快
pǎo de kuài
Pedaling so fast

上面坐个老太太
shàng miàn zuò ge lǎo tài tài
Ridden by an old lady

要五毛给一块
yào wǔ máo gěi yí kuài
I asked for five cents,
she gave me one dollar

你说奇怪不奇怪
nǐ shuō qí guài bù qí guài
How strange is that!

Muffin Man

Oh, do you know the muffin man,
The muffin man, the muffin man,
Oh, do you know the muffin man,
That lives on Drury Lane?

Oh, yes, I know the muffin man,
The muffin man, the muffin man.
Oh, yes, I know the muffin man
That lives on Drury Lane.

Doughnuts for Sale
卖油条
mài yóu tiáo

街头巷尾卖油条
jiē tóu xiàng wěi mài yóu tiáo
Doughnuts for sale along the streets

卖来卖去卖不掉
mài lái mài qù mài bú diào
All day he couldn't sell them

哗啦啦啦啦啦变成老油条
huā lā lā lā lā lā biàn chéng lǎo yóu tiáo
Hua-la-la-la-la-la they all got stale.

Do you know ...

Have you been to a farmers' market where there are people selling fresh fruit and vegetables, meat, fish, and tasty treats? Traditionally, Chinese people go to the market every day to shop for fresh food. Going to the market is fun: you meet neighbors and friends.

Imagine you are planning for your birthday party. Can you find all the things you need at this market?

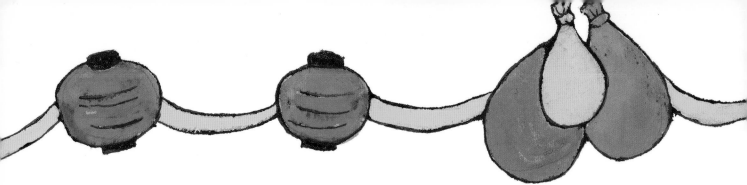

Happy Birthday to You

Happy birthday to you
Happy birthday to you
Happy birthday dear ...
Happy birthday to you.

Do you know ...

It is common that Chinese don't celebrate their children's birthdays every year, but they honor children's one-month-old and one-year-old birthdays. After the first birthday, the next important birthday celebration is at 60 years old.

Noodles and peaches are symbols of long life, so long noodles and peach-shaped steamed buns are served at birthday parties.

Look at the presents brought for the baby's one-month birthday. Can you find the presents for the baby—a pair of gold bracelets from the grandma, four red eggs from the neighbor, a silver necklace from the auntie, and lucky money in a red envelope from the uncle?

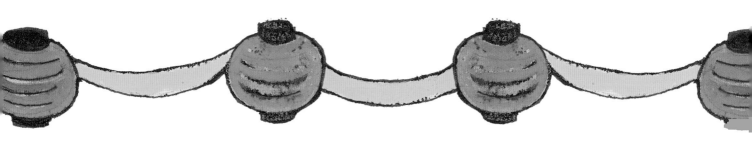

Happy Birthday to You
祝你生日快乐
zhù nǐ shēng rì kuài lè

祝你生日快乐
zhù nǐ shēng rì kuài lè
Happy birthday to you

祝你生日快乐
zhù nǐ shēng rì kuài lè
Happy birthday to you

祝你生日快乐
zhù nǐ shēng rì kuài lè
Happy birthday to you

祝你生日快乐
zhù nǐ shēng rì kuài lè
Happy birthday to you.

21

I'm a Little Teapot

I'm a little teapot
Short and stout
Here is my handle
Here is my spout.

When I get all steamed up
Then I shout
Tip me over and pour me out!

Little Sister

妹妹背着洋娃娃

mèi mei bēi zhe yáng wā wā

妹妹背着洋娃娃
mèi mei bēi zhe yáng wā wā
Little sister carries her baby doll

走到花园来看花
zǒu dào huā yuán lái kàn huā
Walks to the garden to see the flowers

娃娃哭了叫妈妈
wā wā kū le jiào māma
The baby doll cries for its mother

树上小鸟笑哈哈
shù shàng xiǎo niǎo xiào hā hā
The bird laughs from the treetops.

Three Young Rats with Black Felt Hats

Three young rats with black felt hats,
Three young ducks with white straw flats,
Three young dogs with curling tails,
Three young cats with demi–veils.

Went out to walk with two young pigs
In satin vests and sorrel wigs,
But suddenly it chanced to rain,
And so they all went home again.

Do you know ...

More than 2,000 years ago,
Chinese invented the zodiac
animals to keep track of years.
Each year is matched to one of the
12 animals at the top of the page.
Many Chinese still use the zodiac
animals to tell someone their age.

Can you find all of the zodiac
animals in the picture?

24

Two Tigers

两只老虎
liǎng zhī lǎo hǔ

两只老虎, 两只老虎
liǎng zhī lǎo hǔ , liǎng zhī lǎo hǔ
Two tigers, two tigers

跑得快, 跑得快
pǎo de kuài, pǎo de kuài
Run very fast, run very fast

一只没有耳朵
yì zhī méi yǒu ěr duō
One without an ear

一只没有尾巴
yì zhī méi yǒu wěi bā
One without a tail

真奇怪, 真奇怪
zhēn qí guài, zhēn qí guài
How strange, how strange.

The Train
火车快飞
huǒ chē kuài fēi

火车快飞
huǒ chē kuài fēi
The train speeding fast

火车快飞
huǒ chē kuài fē
The train speeding fast

穿过高山
chuān guò gāo shān
Going through the
mountains

渡过小溪
dù guò xiǎo xī
Crossing the rivers

不知穿过几百里
bù zhī chuān guò jǐ bǎi lǐ
How many li it travels!

搭到家里搭到家
dā dào jiā lǐ dā dào jiā lǐ
Taking me home, taking me home

妈妈看见真欢喜
māma kàn jiàn zhēn huān xǐ
Mama is so happy to see me.

26

Do you know ...

A li is about ⅓ of a mile, or 0.5 km.

Down by the Station

Down by the station
Early in the morning
See the little puffer-bellies all in a row.

See the engine driver
Pull the little handle
Chug, chug, poof, poof,
Off we go!

The Moon Is Rising
月亮出来了
yuè liàng chū lái liǎo

月亮出来了
yuè liàng chū lái liǎo
The moon is rising

月亮出来了
yùe lìang chū lái liǎo
The moon is rising

弯弯黄黄挂在椰树梢
wān wān huáng huáng guà zài yé shù shāo
Its crescent yellow shape dangling in the coconut tree

羊儿看见了喜的咩咩叫
yáng er kàn jiàn liǎo xǐ de miē miē jiào
The sheep look at the moon bleating with delight

它喊宝宝快来瞧
tā hǎn bǎo bao kuài lái qiáo
And call their babies to see

椰子树上结香蕉
yé zi shù shàng jié xiāng jiāo
The banana-growing coconut tree.

I See the Moon
I see the moon
And the moon sees me
The moon sees the somebody I'd like to see.
God bless the moon
And God bless me
God bless the somebody I'd like to see!

Little Stars
小星星
xiǎo xīng xīng

一闪一闪亮晶晶
yì shǎn yì shǎn liàng jīng jīng
Twinkling, twinkling, shining bright

满天都是小星星
mǎn tiān dōu shì xiǎo xīng xīng
The sky is full of little stars

高挂天上放光明
gāo guà tiān shàng fàng guāng míng
High up in the sky so bright

好象许多小眼睛
hǎo xiàng xǔ duō xiǎo yǎn jīng
Like many tiny shining eyes.

一闪一闪亮晶晶
yì shǎn yì shǎn liàng jīng jīng
Twinkling, twinkling, shining bright

满天都是小星星
mǎn tiān dōu shì xiǎo xīng xīng
The sky is full of little stars.

Twinkle, Twinkle, Little Star

Twinkle, twinkle, little star
How I wonder what you are
Up above the world so high
Like a diamond in the sky
Twinkle, twinkle little star
How I wonder what you are.

Do you know ...

Chinese people follow the lunar calendar. You can watch this calendar change by looking at the shape of the moon. For example, the full moon means that it is the 15th of the Chinese lunar month.

It's fun to see the moon change its shape over a course of days! Find a time at night to go outside and look at the moon. Draw a picture of it. Do this for at least a week. Compare your drawings.

What do you see?

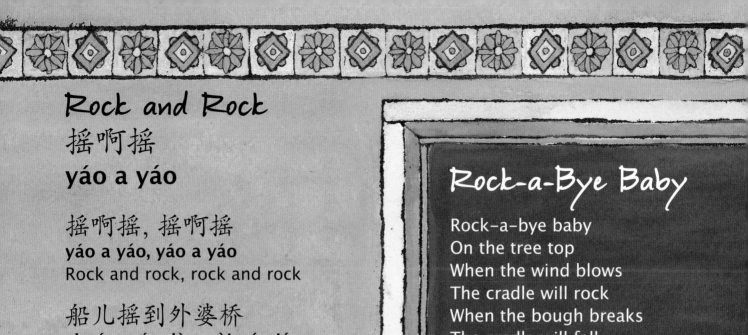

Rock and Rock

摇啊摇
yáo a yáo

摇啊摇, 摇啊摇
yáo a yáo, yáo a yáo
Rock and rock, rock and rock

船儿摇到外婆桥
chuánr yáo dào wài pó qiáo
Rocking the boat to grandma's house

外婆好外婆好
wài pó hǎo, wài pó hǎo
Hello, grandma, hello, grandma

外婆对我嘻嘻笑
wài pó duì wǒ xī xī xiào
Grandma is smiling at me

摇啊摇, 摇啊摇
yáo a yáo, yáo a yáo
Rock and rock, rock and rock

船儿摇到外婆桥
chuánr yáo dào wài pó qiáo
Rocking the boat to grandma's house

外婆说好宝宝
wài pó shuō hǎo bǎo bǎo
Grandma says, good baby

外婆给我一块糕
wài pó gěi wǒ yí kuài gāo
Grandma gives me a treat.

Rock-a-Bye Baby

Rock-a-bye baby
On the tree top
When the wind blows
The cradle will rock
When the bough breaks
The cradle will fall
And down will come baby,
cradle and all.

Star Light, Star Bright

Star light, star bright
First star I see tonight
I wish I may
I wish I might
Have the wish I wish
tonight.

My Mama's Eyes

妈妈的眼睛
māma dē yǎn jīng

美丽的美丽的天空里
měi lì de měi lì de tiān kōng lǐ
Beautiful beautiful sky

出来了光亮的小星星
chū lái liǎo guāng liàng de xiǎo xīng xīng
Little bright stars appearing

好象是我妈妈慈爱的眼睛
hǎo xiàng shì wǒ māma cí ài de yǎn jīng
Like my mama's loving eyes

妈妈的眼睛我最喜爱
māma de yǎn jīng wǒ zuì xǐ ài
I love my mama's eyes

常常希望我做个好小孩
cháng cháng xī wàng wǒ zuò gē hǎo xiǎo hái
She wishes me to be good

妈妈的眼睛我最喜爱
māma de yǎn jīng wǒ zuì xǐ ài
I love my mama's eyes.

About the Chinese Language

Written Chinese

Each Chinese character is pronounced as a single syllable and has its own meaning. Chinese writing was invented about 5,000 years ago. The characters we use today originated as pictograms—that is, drawings that represented things in nature, such as animals, rivers and plants. These written words gradually changed in appearance through the millennia, resulting in today's characters.

There are two systems for writing Chinese characters today. The "traditional" form is more complex. The "simplified" form is more simple and streamlined, and was created by the Chinese government to make reading and writing easier. Many characters are identical in the two forms. This book's Chinese characters are shown in simplified form. To download the rhymes in traditional form characters, please visit www.tuttlepublishing.com.

Spoken Chinese

There are many dialects spoken in China. After 1913, the Mandarin dialect was chosen as the official spoken language in China.

An internationally-recognized phonetic system called pinyin is a way to express the sounds of the Chinese language, and to write them using the characters that English-speakers are more familiar with.

Whether you read the Chinese character or the pinyin equivalent, the sounds of Chinese are somewhat different than those of the English language. Listen to the CD to begin to understand how the Chinese sounds work (and how pinyin expresses them).

Mandarin Chinese is a tonal language, so along with the sounds themselves, each Chinese character also carries a tone.

These are the tone marks used in pinyin. They indicate for you which tone to use when saying a syllable:

- ‾ 1st tone: high and level
- ´ 2nd tone: high and rising
- ˇ 3rd tone: dipping low, then rising again
- ` 4th tone: sharply falling

Sing Along!

Outside

Inside

Party

Play

Night

Bonus Rhymes!

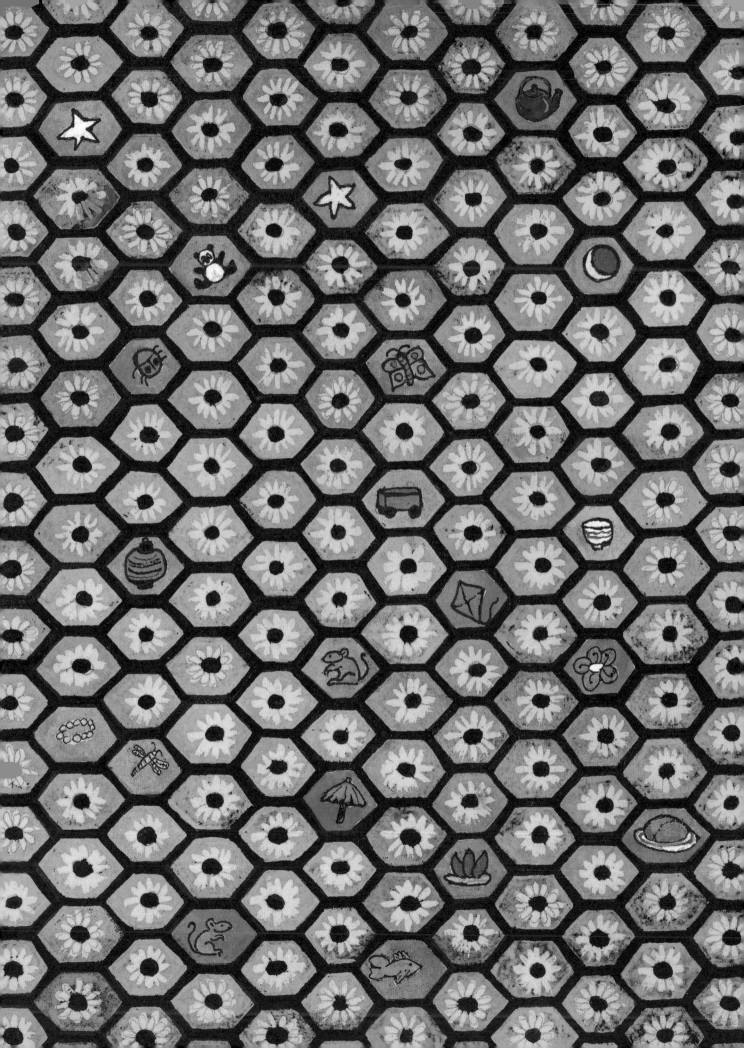

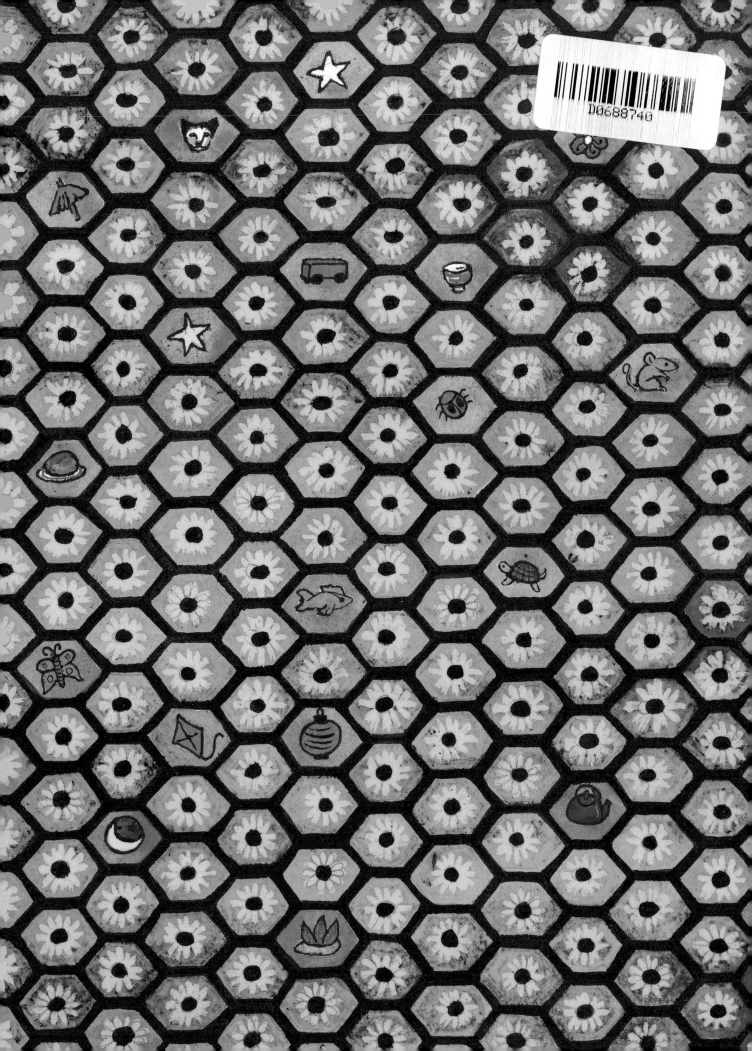

Chinese
and English
Nursery Rhymes

LITTLE MOUSE
AND OTHER CHARMING CHINESE RHYMES

FAYE-LYNN WU
illustrated by
KIEREN DUTCHER

TUTTLE Publishing

Tokyo | Rutland, Vermont | Singapore

ABOUT TUTTLE
"Books to Span the East and West"

Our core mission at Tuttle Publishing is to create books which bring people together one page at a time. Tuttle was founded in 1832 in the small New England town of Rutland, Vermont (USA). Our fundamental values remain as strong today as they were then—to publish best-in-class books informing the English-speaking world about the countries and peoples of Asia. The world has become a smaller place today and Asia's economic, cultural and political influence has expanded, yet the need for meaningful dialogue and information about this diverse region has never been greater. Since 1948, Tuttle has been a leader in publishing books on the cultures, arts, cuisines, languages and literatures of Asia. Our authors and photographers have won numerous awards and Tuttle has published thousands of books on subjects ranging from martial arts to paper crafts. We welcome you to explore the wealth of information available on Asia at **www.tuttlepublishing.com**.

Published by Tuttle Publishing, an imprint of Periplus Editions (HK) Ltd.

www.tuttlepublishing.com

Copyright © 2010 by Faye-Lynn Wu
Illustrations © 2010 by Kieren Dutcher

ISBN 978-0-8048-4999-9
(Previously published as under ISBN 978-0-8048-4094-1, CIP Data No. 2009031567)

First edition
22 21 20 19 18   4 3 2 1   1801EP

Printed in Hong Kong

Distributed by

North America, Latin America & Europe
Tuttle Publishing
364 Innovation Drive
North Clarendon, VT 05759-9436 U.S.A.
Tel: 1 (802) 773-8930
Fax: 1 (802) 773-6993
info@tuttlepublishing.com
www.tuttlepublishing.com

Asia Pacific
Berkeley Books Pte. Ltd.
61 Tai Seng Avenue #02-12
Singapore 534167
Tel: (65) 6280-1330
Fax: (65) 6280-6290
inquiries@periplus.com.sg
www.periplus.com

TUTTLE PUBLISHING® is a registered trademark of Tuttle Publishing, a division of Periplus Editions (HK) Ltd.

To my husband, Alex, and children, Benjamin and Rachel,
for their love, patience, and support.
—FW

To Dan, Sophie and William.
I couldn't have done it without you!
—KD

Our sincere thanks to our family, friends, and colleagues in the CD song production—Madeleine King, a fantastic musician, for her creative songwriting and lovely music; the singers, PJ (Paul) Robinson, Caroline Portante, Adella K. Cho, Cathy (Lan Qi) Li, Shihua Liu, and Hui Qiao Wu; Menna Stern for her technical support; and John Carlstroem and Siu-mui Woo for their support behind the scenes.

Introduction

When my son was born, I read him Mother Goose rhymes and sang my favorite childhood songs in Chinese to ease my own homesickness. Not only did I have fun learning the English rhymes with my son, but I also passed my Chinese heritage down to him through singing and acting out my old favorites. I can still see his sleepy face and hear his childish voice begging for more rhymes: "Sing, mommy, sing."

Children naturally love music and verse, so it is no wonder that nursery rhymes appeal to us as children and stay with us throughout our lives. What could be a more enjoyable way to learn a different culture and language than through rhymes and songs?

Bugs, trains, counting: we've paired the rhymes by shared themes, so for each, there's a Chinese rhyme and an English rhyme to delight in. We invite young readers and adults to explore the magic of children's rhymes and the universal quality of the shared world of childhood. We also provide notes throughout the book so that you can learn more about Chinese culture.

Whether you are a native Chinese speaker or English speaker, you can learn the rhymes and songs—simply follow the words as you sing, or join in the chorus on the audio CD.

Enjoy!

Faye-Lynn Wu and Kieren Dutcher